21st Century Skills Library

LIFE SKILLS BIOGRAPHIES

TIGER WOODS

Lucia Raatma

Cherry Lake Publishing
Ann Arbor, Michigan

Published in the United States of America by Cherry Lake Publishing
Ann Arbor, MI
www.cherrylakepublishing.com

Content Adviser: Lawrence J. Londino, PhD, Chairperson, Broadcasting Department, Montclair State University, Montclair, New Jersey

Photo Credits: Cover and page 1, © Tannen Maury/epa/Corbis; pages 5, 23, 30, and 43, © Reuters/Corbis; page 9, © Chris McPherson/Corbis; page 10, © Christina Salvador/Sygma/Corbis; pages 12 and 14, © Richard Dole/Corbis; page 17, David Madison/NewSport/Corbis; page 18, © The Oregonian/Mike Lloyd/Corbis Sygma; pages 20 and 21, © Kramer Daniel/Corbis Sygma; page 25, © Atlanta Constitution/Corbis Sygma; page 27, © Sue Ogrocki/Reuters/Corbis; page 29, © Matt Campbell/epa/Corbis; page 33, © Toby Melville/Reuters/Corbis; page 35, © Ellen Ozier/Reuters/Corbis; page 36, © Vaughn Youtz/Zuma/Corbis; page 37, © Steven Georges/Corbis; page 42, © Jeff J. Mitchell/Reuters/Corbis

Library of Congress Cataloging-in-Publication Data
Raatma, Lucia.
 Tiger Woods / by Lucia Raatma.
  p. cm. — (Life skills biographies)
 ISBN-13: 978-1-60279-076-6
 ISBN-10: 1-60279-076-0
 1. Woods, Tiger—Juvenile literature. 2. Golfers—United States—Biography—Juvenile literature.
I. Title. II. Series.
 GV964.W66R33 2008
 796.352092—dc22
 [B]   2007006969

*Cherry Lake Publishing would like to acknowledge the work of
The Partnership for 21st Century Skills.
Please visit* www.21stcenturyskills.org *for more information.*

Contents

Introduction   4

CHAPTER ONE
From the Beginning   5

CHAPTER TWO
A Young Phenomenon   12

CHAPTER THREE
The Professional Game   20

CHAPTER FOUR
Giving Back   35

CHAPTER FIVE
The Tiger Woods Legacy   40

Timeline   44

Glossary   46

For More Information   47

Index   48

About the Author   48

Introduction

When many people think of golf, they think of Tiger Woods. He is one of the most successful golfers ever and one of the most recognized faces in the world.

What makes Tiger Woods so successful and so appealing? Well, he has talent—that's for sure. But talent is never enough. He also has determination and drive and willpower and respect for other people. These qualities have made him a great golfer and a great person.

❧

CHAPTER ONE

FROM THE BEGINNING

Earl and Kultida Woods watch as their son, Tiger, is presented the ceremonial green jacket after winning the 2002 Masters tournament.

Eldrick "Tiger" Woods was born on December 30, 1975, in Southern California. He grew up in the town of Cypress, which is near Los Angeles. The Civil Rights Act of 1964 had been signed, but unfortunately, **discrimination** was far from over in the 1970s. Many people still feared those with different racial backgrounds. And Tiger's background is a mixed one. His father, Earl, was Native American, Chinese, Caucasian, and African American. And his mother, Kultida, is part Caucasian, Thai, and Chinese.

His parents met in Thailand when Earl was serving in the U.S. Army during the Vietnam War (mid-1950s–1975). Kultida (known as Tida) was working as a receptionist in an office that Earl had to visit on military business. The story goes that he asked her out, and they were to meet at nine. When Tida didn't show up that night, Earl assumed she wasn't interested. But she and her chaperone were looking for him the next morning. Tida assumed the date was for the morning, since going out at night would have been inappropriate in her culture.

After that rocky start, the two became a couple. They came to the United States and, in 1969, were married. Earl spent a few more years in the army and then retired in 1974. He had been married before and had three children with his first wife. In hopes of having a closer relationship with them, Earl and Tida Woods moved to California.

Earl Woods wasn't sure he wanted to have more children, but Tida insisted. They had a son and named him Eldrick—a name that started with E for Earl and ended with K for Kultida. But he was called Tiger from an early age. When Earl was in the Vietnam War, he had become good friends with a Vietnamese soldier who had saved his life more than once. Earl nicknamed this soldier Tiger, after the fiercest animal in the jungle. And he remembered this friend by nicknaming his son Tiger. Earl saw Tiger's birth as a second chance for him. He wanted to be a big part of his son's life and raise him to be a remarkable person.

THE YOUNG GOLFER

Earl Woods was a good athlete. He'd played baseball in college and even thought about turning pro. In his 40s, he took up the game of golf. He had a good swing and understood the basics of the game. But golf is a tough sport and requires lots of practice. So Earl would spend hours in his garage, hitting golf balls into a net or practicing his putts. And sometimes, he'd bring little Tiger with him.

Sitting in his baby seat, Tiger would watch his father. While most children might have fallen asleep or played with toys, Tiger really seemed to watch his father practice. One day when Tiger was nine months old and hardly able to walk, he picked up a golf club that Earl had shortened for him and swung it. By the time he was just 18 months old, he was going with his father to the local driving range, where players practice their drives, which are the long shots in golf.

Earl played at the navy golf couse, and soon Tiger started going along. The child learned the game quickly and enjoyed working on his skills. Lots of people

At professional golf matches, the fans are often told to be really quiet when the players tee off, or hit their first shot, or when they putt on the green. Golf is a game that requires concentration, and any noise can be a distraction. Both Earl and Tiger knew that no golf course was going to be quiet all the time. A plane might go over, or a child might cry. So early on, Earl worked with Tiger to strengthen his concentration. As Earl explained, "I pulled every nasty, dirty, rambunctious, obnoxious trick on my son week after week after week. I dropped a bag of clubs at impact of his swing. I imitated a crow's voice while he was stroking a putt. When he was about ready to hit a shot, I would toss a ball right in front of his." It was up to Tiger to ignore all these outside distractions and focus on the task at hand.

noticed this toddler playing golf, and he caught the attention of a sports journalist. This led to Tiger appearing on the *Mike Douglas Show*, a popular talk show at the time, when he was just two years old. Comedian and avid golfer Bob Hope was on, too, and they were planning to putt some golf balls. Hope asked Tiger if he had any money, suggesting they might place bets on who'd win. So Tiger picked up his ball and placed it closer to the cup. Then he tapped it in, and the audience roared with laughter. Even as a toddler, Tiger was a crowd-pleaser.

When he was five, Tiger was featured in *Golf Digest* magazine. And he appeared on the TV show *That's Incredible*. This young athlete was capturing a lot of attention.

It was obvious that Tiger had a gift for the game. In fact, he was only six years old when he shot his first hole in one on a regulation golf course. It wasn't long before Earl and Tida had to find professionals to help their son sharpen his skills. One early coach was Rudy Duran, with the Heartwell Golf Course in Long Beach. Duran was amazed when he saw Tiger swing. "He was like a shrunken touring pro," he remembered. Another coach, John Anselmo, started teaching Tiger when he was about 10 years old. "I saw so much rhythm and balance, even when he was 10," Anselmo says. "I was awed by it."

GROWING UP

Earl and Tida Woods knew their son was special, but they didn't want that going to his head. They were determined that he would be a regular

Rudy Duran was one of Tiger's first golf coaches.

kid who went to school and studied and played with his friends. So Tiger attended the local public schools. And early on, his parents emphasized earning good grades. In fact, there was a rule that Tiger couldn't play golf until his homework was done. And if he misbehaved, the golf clubs were taken away. For Tiger, that was the worst punishment.

There were times when Tiger was mistreated because of his racial background. On his first day of kindergarten, a group of mostly white

Tiger Woods excelled at golf from an early age, but his parents also made sure that he earned good grades.

older boys tied him to a tree. They teased him and called him racist names. The incident may have frightened Tiger, but he kept going to the school. And overall, his experiences in public school were good.

He did well in other sports, too, such as basketball and running. But ultimately, Tiger quit those to concentrate on golf. When he was eight years old, he won the Optimist International Junior tournament. And he repeated that win five times. He won scores of local tournaments as well. In fact, in 1987, he finished first in more than 30 tournaments in Southern California. By the age of 14, Tiger had at least 200 golf trophies.

Jack Nicklaus was a champion golfer for many years, and Tiger has called Nicklaus his role model. Nicklaus inspired Tiger to set goals and work hard to meet them. When Tiger was a young boy, he created a chart that he hung on his wall. In one column, he wrote a list of all the major golf championships (the U.S. Open, British Open, Masters, and PGA Championship). He pasted a photo of Jack Nicklaus on the chart. And in the other column, he listed Nicklaus's age when he won each of the tournaments. Tiger set his mind to winning those titles—and doing it at a younger age than Nicklaus did. That was his goal. Then he went to work to accomplish it.

CHAPTER TWO

A Young Phenomenon

While Tiger Woods was in high school, his success on the golf course continued. When he was 15, he entered the U.S. Junior Amateur Championship, run by the United States Golf Association (USGA). This is a tournament open to players ages 18 and younger. He won the title. No one his age had ever done that.

Tiger Woods celebrates his first USGA Junior Golf Championship win with his father.

Tiger's success at this level piqued the interest of several **sports agents** who wanted him as a client. Mark McCormack of International Management Group (IMG) was one of them. But because Tiger was still an amateur, a ranking in the sport that meant he could not accept any kind of money for his golfing expenses, this was not possible. So McCormack did the next best thing. He signed Earl Woods on as a consultant who would scout out promising young golfers at all the tournaments he attended. This job was a great solution for everyone. Earl and Tida Woods were spending a lot of money to have their son play golf. By one estimate, they laid out $30,000 a year for his coaching and tournament appearances. So the extra money from IMG was welcomed.

WORKING ON HIS GAME

During his teenage years, Tiger turned from a skinny kid to a tall, toned athlete. As he grew, he had to make adjustments to how he played the game. One person who helped out was Butch Harmon, a noted swing coach. Harmon worked with Tiger in person to analyze and improve the way he swung the golf club. The two also sent videos back and forth and talked on the phone. All the work helped Tiger land a second win at the U.S. Junior Amateur Championship when he was 16. He was the first person to win the title two years in a row.

His success as an amateur caught the attention of the Professional Golfers Association (PGA). That group invited Tiger to play in the 1992 Los Angeles Open. Most of the players in this tournament would be pros, but a few amateurs were allowed to play as well. This was big news. At 16,

Tiger would be the youngest golfer ever to play in a PGA Tour event in the United States. He didn't win, but he did score a **birdie** on the first hole. So he got to see his name at the top of the **leaderboard** for a little while. It was a fun event for Tiger. And by the end of it, he had a whole new group of fans.

At 17, Tiger entered the U.S. Junior Amateur Championship again. He had just gone through a growth spurt and had recently recovered from mononucleosis (a disease caused by a virus). But he didn't let that

Young Tiger Woods lines up a putt.

stop him. In the finals, he faced a talented player named Ryan Armour. Most amateur tournaments are designed as match play, where two golfers compete against each other, one-on-one. (This differs from most professional tournaments.) In match play, every hole is a separate contest, so each hole has a winner. The winner of the game is the player who has won the most holes. Ryan had played well all day and was two holes ahead of Tiger, with just two holes left to play. But in the end, Tiger made two birdies on those last two holes. So at the end of 18 holes, the two young men were tied. They went into a **sudden-death playoff**. And on that first hole, Tiger made **par**. Ryan, amazed that he'd lost his great lead, made a **bogey**. Tiger won his third U.S. Junior Amateur Championship, a record some say is unbreakable.

In the summer of 1994, Tiger Woods played in and won the Western Amateur tournament, and soon after, he was playing in the U.S. Amateur tournament. He had played in the tournament before and had always done well against the older players. But that year, at 18, Woods really hoped to win it. In the preliminary round, he was losing to Buddy Alexander, the golf coach from the University of Florida. With just five holes left, he was three holes down. But Woods made some amazing shots and ended up beating Alexander. From there, he easily got to the finals, where he faced Trip Kuehne, a star from the University of Oklahoma. At one point, Kuehne had built up a six-hole lead, but Woods did not give up. He took it one hole at a time and caught up to Kuehne. Woods birdied the 17th hole and won the tournament. He was the youngest player to ever capture the U.S. Amateur title.

When Tiger was young, his mother, who is a Buddhist, taught him to meditate. This practice requires discipline and perseverance. But it taught him how to stay focused. This ability has helped him in the most challenging of times—both on and off the course.

COLLEGE PLAYER

Several colleges had been hoping to recruit Woods to their teams for many years, including the University of Nevada at Las Vegas and Stanford University in Palo Alto, California. So he had to choose among a number of offers. Ultimately, he chose Stanford, one of the finest universities in the country.

When he started college in September 1994, Woods discovered that he loved campus life. He established a group of good friends, and he enjoyed being on his own. He worked hard in his classes and excelled on the golf team. In fact, he'd already won his first college tournament before classes even began.

But all was not perfect at Stanford. Woods was once mugged on campus, and the thief knew Tiger's name. Whether that attack was a racist one is unclear. But Woods received a number of threatening letters while he was in school.

HIS FIRST MASTERS TOURNAMENT

One of the most prestigious tournaments is the Masters, which is held at Augusta National Golf Course in Augusta, Georgia. Like many other country clubs at the time, this one allowed people to become

Tiger Woods (standing, 4th from left) poses for a picture with the Stanford University golf team in 1994.

members only by invitation. And the club had no black members. Because of his U.S. Amateur win, Woods was invited to play in the 1995 Masters. He was excited at the opportunity but wondered how he would be treated. At some other tournaments, he had received death threats, though he tried not to let this bother him. At the Masters, Woods was welcomed by the other players, and he shot a respectable par for the first two rounds of the tournament. He was the only amateur to make the **cut**. Then he finished the tournament tied for 41st.

When he was a young player, Tiger Woods once fell behind in a tournament, and he seemed to just stop trying. He didn't focus, and his putting was off. When the tournament was over, his father yelled at him—loudly, so people nearby had no trouble hearing. Earl wasn't angry that Tiger lost. He was furious because Tiger just quit. Tiger Woods learned an important lesson that day. No matter who is winning, he can never stop trying. He now takes the game one shot at a time and always gives his best.

GAINING MORE EXPERIENCE

In 1995, Tiger Woods entered the U.S. Amateur tournament as the favorite. He didn't disappoint. In the early rounds, he dominated his opponents. And in the final round, he trailed by three holes. But he overcame that and won the title for the second time. That year, he also played in the British Open and a variety of other tournaments.

Woods began to see how he had to work on all parts of

Tiger Woods won the U.S. Amateur tournament three times.

his game if he was going to succeed at the professional level. He needed: long drives for good placement in the **fairway**; medium shots to get him on the green; and putts that were firm and accurate. He realized he had to get stronger. So back at Stanford in the fall of 1995, he worked out with weights. All his hours in the weight room helped him make longer **tee shots**. And that long-ball strength has proven key to his success on the golf course.

In the summer of 1996, Woods returned to the U.S. Amateur tournament and made history. In the final against Steve Scott, Woods found himself behind by five holes. But he took it hole by hole and soon came back and made it a tie. The two young men entered a sudden-death playoff, and Woods won the title. He is the only person to have won the amateur championship three times.

Tiger Woods knew that his future could be an amazing one. He enjoyed college, but he believed it was time to move on. It was time to turn pro.

CHAPTER THREE

THE PROFESSIONAL GAME

Tiger Woods speaks to the press in 1996.

When Tiger Woods became a professional golfer, the whole world was watching. And many companies wanted him to be a spokesperson for their products. Woods did not take these offers lightly. He knew he could make a lot of money from **endorsements**. But he also knew that his name would be used to sell products. So he chose carefully.

Woods initially agreed to work with Nike, a maker of athletic shoes, equipment, and clothing, and Titleist, a company known for its golf balls. Since then, he has endorsed products for other companies including American Express and General Motors. These companies get to use Woods's name and face on their products. In return, they provide him with money so he can train and participate in tournaments. Nearly the minute he turned pro, Woods was a millionaire many times over.

Tiger Woods shows off his Nike golf shoes.

ON THE PGA TOUR

Tiger Woods didn't win his first tournament as a professional, but he gained lots of fans. Professional tournaments are designed as stroke play, so a player's total number of shots per round is the player's score. At the Greater Milwaukee Open, he shot an impressive 67 on his first day. And he wowed spectators with a hole in one on the last day of the tournament. With his now-famous pumping fist, he celebrated that great feat. But he ended up tied for 60th place.

In his next three tournaments, Woods had good days and bad days. He finished 11th at the Canadian Open. Then he blew a lead at the Quad City Classic and tied for fifth. Then he came in third at the B.C. Open. He had played in four professional tournaments, one after another. He didn't realize how demanding the schedule would be, and he was exhausted.

ADMITTING MISTAKES

In September 1996, Woods was scheduled to play in the Buick Challenge in Pine Mountain, Georgia, and he was to be honored at the Fred Haskins Award dinner as the top college player of the year. But he

Tiger Woods pumps his fist to celebrate sinking a putt.

was tired from the four tournaments he had just played—and from all the traveling. So he withdrew from the tournament and didn't attend the dinner. The tournament organizers were furious. So were the people who had planned the dinner. Woods didn't realize how much people had been counting on him.

As soon as he understood what he had done, he took responsibility for his actions. He wrote an article for *Golf World* magazine and tried to explain himself: "I do make mistakes. . . . I'm only twenty years old and this is all new to me. . . . I realize now that what I did was wrong." Woods also wrote a letter of apology to everyone who had planned to attend the dinner. He learned that people had come to rely on him, and he has been careful ever since not to let them down.

LEARNING THE ROPES

By October, Woods was rested and ready to play in the Las Vegas Invitational. His scores improved each day of this competition, and he entered the final day four shots down. But he made a comeback and caught leader Davis Love III. At the end of 18 holes, the score was tied. The two men entered a playoff, and Woods emerged victorious. He had his first PGA win.

A few weeks later, Woods won another event, making it two PGA victories in just his first seven tries. Fans loved him, and tournament organizers wanted him in their lineups.

Woods was learning more about his game and more about himself. If something in his game didn't seem right, he was willing to make changes. He worked with swing coach Butch Harmon to improve his technique. When it was time for the 1997 Masters, Woods thought he was prepared.

On the first day of the Masters tournament, Woods got off to a slow start. In fact, he made four bogeys on the first nine holes. But he took time to refocus. He remembered what his father had said about quitting. Then,

*Tiger Woods puts on the traditional green jacket
after winning the 1997 Masters tournament.*

as he put it, "I finally decided to play some golf." On the second nine holes of that first day, he shot four birdies and an **eagle**. He ended that day with a score of 70, just three strokes off the lead. The next day, he shot a 66 and was the tournament leader by three shots. By the end of the third day, he had built a nine-stroke lead, and the golf world was buzzing.

On the last day of the tournament, people from all over the world watched as Woods broke records. He won the tournament by 12 strokes, the biggest margin in the history of the tournament. He also set the Masters record for lowest score, a total of 270 for 72 holes. He became its

Tiger Woods understands that other players have made his success possible. Lee Elder was the first African American to play at the Masters. Charlie Sifford and Ted Rhodes were professional golfers who were not allowed to play in most major events because they were black. When Woods earned his historic win at the Masters, he thanked them for all they had done for the game of golf. He told reporters, "I am the first minority to win here, but I wasn't the first to play. That was Lee Elder, and my hat's off to him and Charlie Sifford and Ted Rhodes, who made this possible for me."

youngest winner (at age 21) and the youngest winner of any major since 1922. He was thrilled to be presented with the traditional green jacket that every Masters champion receives. And Tiger Woods became the first person of color to own it.

THE CHALLENGE OF BEING FAMOUS

After Woods won the 1997 Masters, he was in even greater demand. People wanted him to make appearances at a variety of events. He was featured on the covers of magazines and made even more commercials for his sponsors. Finding time for himself and trying to keep the game fun were challenges for the young golfer. The rest of 1997 was bumpy for Woods. His finishes at the other major tournaments were not great: U.S. Open (19th), British Open (24th), and PGA Championship (29th). Woods was proving that, though he is a great player, he is not superhuman.

By the end of that year, Woods also began to analyze his game. He thought he was swinging too hard, and he asked Harmon to help him change

Coach Butch Harmon works with Tiger Woods to help improve his swing.

All too often, TV gossip shows and tabloid newspapers are filled with celebrities who are behaving badly. Though easily recognizable and often in the public eye, Woods has never let his fame go to his head. He doesn't need to show off for the cameras or do ridiculous things for more attention. He knows he is responsible for his actions.

his swing. Harmon warned that changing a swing can lead to other problems on the golf course. And he said it was not a quick and easy process. Woods didn't mind that. He was determined to change his swing for the better.

During 1998, Woods continued to work on his swing. And Harmon's warnings were valid. Woods did not win any majors that year. Many fans were

Tiger Woods has been careful to surround himself with good advisers and friends. And he appreciates the help he gets from them. As Woods's caddie, Steve Williams sometimes offers advice on a shot. And he remembers one example of Woods giving credit where it was due: "He had a difficult putt on the 17th hole of the final round in the 1999 PGA Championship at Medinah, the day he and Sergio Garcia were fighting it out. Tiger's putt was an eight-footer he needed, and he made it by hitting it firm, left side. He won, and that Christmas, he sent me a picture with him holding the trophy, signed, 'Nice read on No. 17, Stevie.' That meant a lot."

disappointed, and they wondered what had happened to his game. Many commentators began to suggest that maybe Woods was not the player everyone thought he was.

The next year, as he worked on his game, Woods decided to make another change—to get a new **caddie**. He looked for someone smart and helpful, who could also handle the big crowds and stay loyal to him. So Woods asked Steve Williams, a New Zealander, to be his caddie. The two have been together ever since.

That year, Woods began to get back in the groove. He won the PGA Championship in an incredible battle against Sergio Garcia. This was his second PGA major win. He went on to win each of the next four PGA tournaments he entered. It seemed that Woods had made the right changes after all.

A REMARKABLE YEAR

As 2000 began, Woods continued to win. He was victorious in the first two tournaments of the year (the Mercedes Championships and the National Pro-Am). His six-win streak tied one that golfing great Ben Hogan had attained in 1948.

In April 2000, Woods was disappointed with his performance at the Masters. But that June, he was amazing at the U.S. Open. This tournament is played at a different course each year. This particular year, it was on the famed course at Pebble Beach in northern California. Wind made play difficult, but that didn't bother Woods. He ended up winning the title by 15 strokes, a tournament record. And the final day of the tournament is always Father's Day. Even though his father wasn't there, Woods knew he had given him a great present. For Woods, that victory was magical.

Steve Williams (right) became Tiger Woods' caddie in 1999.

*Tiger Woods talks to Jack Nicklaus at the PGA
Championship tournament in 2000.*

The next month, he headed to the St. Andrews course in Scotland for the British Open. Golf has been played at St. Andrews for more than 450 years, so playing there is special. The course is very windy, which makes play difficult. But again, Woods didn't let the wind or the **bunkers** bother him. He won, and his final score was a record 19 strokes under par. By capturing that title, he had now won each of the major tournaments. Only four other professional players have ever done this: Jack Nicklaus, Ben Hogan, Gary Player, and Gene Sarazen. (Bobby Jones actually won four major tournaments in one year, 1930. But the tournaments that were considered the majors then were different, and he played as an amateur.)

The final major of that year was the PGA Championship. And it proved to be a special one. In the first two rounds, Woods was paired with legend Jack Nicklaus. Nicklaus had said this would be his last PGA Championship, so Woods was honored to be playing with him. The two enjoyed talking to one another as they walked from hole to hole. And they both scored birdies on the final hole. Nicklaus did not make the cut that Friday, but for both men it was an important round of golf. Woods went on to score a victory in a thrilling three-hole playoff against Bob May. He had won three majors in one year!

The following spring, Tiger Woods continued his amazing run by winning the 2001 Masters. He became the first to hold all four major titles at one time. If someone wins all the majors in the same calendar year, many call it achieving a Grand Slam. Since he didn't win all four titles in one calendar year, it was not a true Grand Slam. But some reporters called it a Tiger Slam.

In 2002, Woods captured the title at the U.S. Open. That victory set another

Tournament play can be exhausting. Golfers fly from city to city, often playing in tournaments several weekends in a row. Most events last four days, from Thursday through Sunday. And players have to practice on the other days. After completing 18 holes in one round of a tournament, most players take time to relax and have dinner. But more often than not, Tiger Woods heads to the gym or practice range. He believes he can never let up, so working out after a full day of golf is something he often pushes himself to do. He also spends hours working on his putts. And early in the morning or late in the evening, he's often seen at the driving range practicing his swing and his long drives. In a January 2007 interview at the Buick Invitational, which Woods won, he commented, "You've always got work to do. That's the name of this game."

record: he became the first person to have won the U.S. Junior Amateur Championship, the U.S. Amateur Championship, and the U.S. Open at least twice each.

UPS AND DOWNS

In 2003, Woods had a disappointing year. He won no major titles, but he did win five PGA tournaments. That made him the first person to have won at least five PGA events each year for five consecutive years. The following year was also a difficult one. He temporarily lost his number-one ranking but still continued to hold his own at PGA events. In 2004, he became the all-time money winner on the PGA tour (with $45 million earned).

When he wasn't playing golf, Woods spent time with close friends. He also had begun seeing Elin Nordegren, a young woman who had been a nanny for golfer Jesper Parnevik. Parnevik introduced the two in 2001, and they began dating soon after. On October 5, 2004, the couple was married at an exclusive golf resort in Barbados.

During this time, some fans and commentators complained about Woods's slump. They wondered if he would continue to dominate the game as he had before. They also wondered if his recent marriage was interfering with his ability to focus on the golf course. Woods ignored all the speculation and roared back in 2005 with a win at the Buick Invitational. He then went on to win the Masters tournament that year. Later that year, he also won the British Open, which was another milestone. He became only the second player to have won all four majors at least twice. Jack Nicklaus is the other.

A Terrible Loss

Tiger Woods had always gained strength from the support of his parents. They sacrificed time and money to provide for him as an amateur. And they continued to offer him advice when he was a professional. At tournaments, one or both parents could usually be seen cheering him on from the sidelines. So it was hard for him when his father's health began failing. More and more frequently, Earl Woods had to stay home and watch events on TV.

When Earl Woods died from cancer in May 2006, Tiger was devastated. This man who had passed on his love of golf—who had been his inspiration from the start—was suddenly gone. Woods tried to focus on his game, but

Tiger Woods met his wife, Elin Nordegren, in 2001.

it was difficult. The next month, he played in the U.S. Open and missed the cut. This was a rare occurrence for this golfing phenomenon. Up until this time, he had made the cut at 142 consecutive tournaments over a span of seven years—a record. Since turning professional, this was the first time he hadn't made the cut at a major tournament.

WINNING AGAIN

But Woods was not one to stay down for long. After all, his father taught him to never quit. He went on to win the last two majors of the year: the British Open and the PGA Championship. That brought his total number of major titles to 12. In August of that year, he also won the Buick Open, which marked his 50th PGA tournament win. At 30, he became the youngest golfer to hit this milestone. Jack Nicklaus accomplished it at 33.

At the end of 2006, Woods was in the midst of another winning streak. At that time, some wondered if he would break the all-time record held by golfing legend Byron Nelson. (Nelson won 11 PGA tournaments in a row.) But he didn't. And, the following summer, he and his wife welcomed their first child, a daughter named Sam Alexis.

What does the future hold for Tiger Woods? And what other records will he break? Will he pass Jack Nicklaus's record 18 wins at the majors? Will he ever win all four majors in one year? Only time will tell.

CHAPTER FOUR

GIVING BACK

What does a true champion do with all of his money and fame? He gives back. In 1996, the same year he turned pro, Tiger Woods and his father established the Tiger Woods Foundation. The organization's goal is to inspire young people and help them be the best they can be. As Woods explains, "From early childhood I dreamed of being the world's best golfer. I worked hard and applied my family's values to everything I did. Integrity,

Tiger Woods instructs a young golfer at a clinic sponsored by the Tiger Woods Foundation.

honesty, discipline, responsibility, and fun; I learned these values at home and in school, each one pushing me further toward my dream. . . . My father and I established the Tiger Woods Foundation to inspire dreams in America's youth because I believe in passing on the values I received from my parents and teachers."

Tiger Woods is dedicated to helping young people achieve their goals.

THE TIGER WOODS LEARNING CENTER

The Tiger Woods Foundation is involved in a number of projects, and one of them is the Tiger Woods Learning Center. Located in Southern California, this center helps students learn beyond the classroom in subjects such as science, language arts, and math. It also provides career guidance in fields such as forensic science, video production, and engineering. The center was dedicated in February 2006, and former president Bill Clinton helped celebrate its opening.

This high-tech, solar-powered center is 35,000 square feet (3,252 square meters) and has 100 computer stations. There is a 200-seat auditorium, seven classrooms, and a café. It is located a few miles from where Woods grew up. It also boasts a driving range and an 18-hole putting course.

When speaking of the center, Woods said, "This is bigger than golf. This is bigger than anything I've done on the golf course, because we will be able to shape lives."

START SOMETHING

Another foundation project, which began in 2000, is called Start Something. This program encourages young people, ages 8 to 17, to identify their personal goals and then find ways to achieve them. After completing the program, participants are eligible to receive academic scholarships. Since the program began, it has given out more than $1 million in scholarships. And it has fueled the dreams of more than 3 million young people.

During his first Masters tournament in 1995, Woods took time to hold a clinic for kids at a local public golf course. He was eager to tell them about the sport and give them some tips. He also took time to speak to a group of African American caddies who worked at Augusta National Golf Course. During this talk, the caddies asked Woods if he thought a person of color could ever win the Masters. Woods said that it would happen. As a matter of fact, he guaranteed it. By taking time to teach the kids and talk to the caddies, he showed that he had respect for people from all walks of life. And he gave them hope for their futures.

OTHER PROGRAMS

Tiger Woods wants to bring the game of golf to kids who might not normally have the chance to play it. The Tiger Woods Foundation National Junior Golf Team does just that. It helps children improve their golf skills and play in international competitions. Since it began, many participants have received full or partial scholarships to colleges throughout the country.

Tiger Woods poses with a group of kids after winning the Target World Challenge tournament in 2006. Woods donated his winnings of more than $1 million to the Tiger Woods Foundation.

The Tiger Woods Foundation also provides financial support to health and educational programs that are designed for children ages 5 to 17. Additionally, the foundation offers a number of scholarships to college-bound students each year.

The foundation has two major fund-raisers. One is a golf tournament that features some of the finest players on the PGA tour. The other is Tiger Jam, a benefit concert held in Las Vegas each year. It has featured performers such as Celine Dion, Christina Aguilera, and Stevie Wonder.

Throughout his career, Woods has acknowledged that he got where he is through hard work and with guidance from the people around him. So he believes it is his duty to take what he knows and pass it along to young people. He has been very successful and very fortunate, and he is more than happy to give back to his community.

Tiger Woods is rich and famous. But he is quick to remember who his friends are. The week after winning the 2000 U.S. Open, he did something unusual. He caddied for a good friend, Jerry Chang, who was trying to qualify for an amateur competition. Imagine how surprised the crowd was to see this champion lugging a heavy bag of clubs for someone else.

In 2002, Woods did a favor for his caddie, Steve Williams. He played in the New Zealand Open on the course where Williams had played as a kid. He also went to a fund-raising dinner for Williams's foundation. As Williams explains, "We're a small country, New Zealand. Muhammad Ali came there, but not to fight. Jack Nicklaus has been down there to fish, but nobody like Tiger ever went there to play golf."

THE TIGER WOODS LEGACY

Tiger Woods has inspired many kids to learn how to play golf.

For many years, especially in the United States, golf had been a sport played by middle-aged wealthy people at country clubs. Some of those clubs didn't let minorities and women become members. So while golf was popular, it was usually most popular with the people who could afford— and were allowed—to play it.

An interesting thing happened when Tiger Woods began dominating the game. Young people began flocking to golf courses. The fans who followed Woods at tournaments were young and old, rich and poor. Kids from all racial backgrounds suddenly thought, "If Tiger can do it, maybe I can, too."

CHANGING THE GAME

Tiger Woods has changed the business and game of golf. When he is playing in a tournament, TV ratings are consistently up. If he chooses not to play in a tournament, attendance at that event is sometimes down. That is a huge responsibility for any athlete. He is often criticized if he chooses not to play an event, since people are relying on him to make the tournament great. But as Woods gets older, he may want to spend more time with his family. So he may not appear at as many events as he has in the past.

Woods is known for having incredibly long tee shots. It is not uncommon for his to travel more than 300 yards (274 m). Because of his skill, some golf course designers are

Being a leader has sometimes been a challenge for Woods. Early on, some people expected him to take a stand when other players or people were discriminated against. For instance, when the topic of women not being allowed to play at some country clubs arose in the media, everyone waited for Woods to take a side. But he chose to stay out of the argument.

And early on, players and fans expected him to take a leadership role on the team of golfers who play in the Ryder Cup, which is a competition between a team from the United States and a team from Europe. But Woods reminded everyone that he was young and the team had more seasoned players who should be the leaders. Now, years later, he is one of the team's more experienced players, and he is taking the rookies under his wing.

One of Tiger Woods's future projects is designing golf courses, which will require much creativity. Tiger Woods Design was founded in November 2006, and the company's plans include building courses all over the world. The company's approach to building the courses is innovative because it wants to design courses that both challenge players and preserve the existing natural environment.

Tiger Woods and teammate Phil Mickelson shake hands at the opening ceremony for the 2004 Ryder Cup Matches.

rethinking how courses are laid out. They never dreamed that a player could master their courses as well as he has.

On the golf course, Woods still has a number of goals for himself. He would like to see more success for the U.S. Ryder Cup team. His record as a player on that team has not been too impressive. In years to come, he will no doubt become a leader on that team and push for international dominance.

Also, Woods is still gunning to break Jack Nicklaus's record of 18 major wins. And who knows what other records he may shatter.

Personally, Tiger Woods is eager to be a good father. He cherished the relationship he had with his dad, and he wants to have the same connection with his own children. Given his determination and drive, those goals are all within reach.

Tiger Woods poses with four of his championship trophies in 2003.

Timeline

1975   Eldrick "Tiger" Woods is born on December 30, in Southern California.

1978   Tiger appears on the *Mike Douglas Show* and putts with comedian Bob Hope.

1981   Tiger is featured in *Golf Digest* magazine and on TV's *That's Incredible*.

1984   Tiger wins the Optimist International Junior tournament at age 8 (he would go on to repeat that win five more times, at ages 9, 12, 13, 14, and 15).

1991   At 15, Tiger becomes the youngest winner of the U.S. Junior Amateur Championship (he wins the title again at ages 16 and 17).

1992   Tiger plays in the Los Angeles Open, his first appearance on the PGA Tour.

1994   At age 18, Woods wins the U.S. Amateur (he repeats this feat in 1995 and 1996). He enrolls at Stanford University after accepting a golf scholarship.

1995   Woods plays in the Masters tournament and ties for 41st; he is the only amateur to make the cut. He is named Stanford's Male Freshman of the Year and first team college All-American.

1996   Woods is named Sportsman of the Year by *Sports Illustrated*. He wins the NCAA Championship. He is named the Fred Haskins College Player of the Year. After winning his third U.S. Amateur Championship, he decides to become a professional golfer. He and his father establish the Tiger Woods Foundation.

1997   Woods wins the Masters, becoming the youngest player and the first player of color to do so; he sets a Masters record with a 12-stroke victory. He becomes the number-one player in the world, in his 42nd week as a professional.

1998   Woods has an "off" year and wins just one PGA event, the BellSouth Classic.

1999   Woods wins his first PGA Championship.

2000   Woods wins the U.S. Open, British Open, and PGA Championship.

2001 Woods wins the Masters, becoming the first player to hold all four major titles at once.

2002 Woods wins his third Masters and his second U.S. Open title. He becomes the first person to win two or more titles at the U.S. Open, U.S. Amateur, and U.S. Junior Amateur tournaments.

2003 Woods wins five PGA tournaments (out of 18 he entered) but no majors; he becomes the first player to have won at least five PGA Tour events each year for five consecutive years.

2004 Woods becomes the career money leader on the PGA tour (with a total of $45 million). He marries Elin Nordegren on October 5.

2005 Woods breaks his slump by winning the Buick Invitational. He wins his fourth Masters title and his second British Open; joins Jack Nicklaus as being the only two players to win all four majors at least twice.

2006 Woods mourns the death of his father, Earl Woods, in May. He misses the cut at the U.S. Open. He wins the British Open. He wins the Buick Open in August, becoming (at 30) the youngest player to win 50 PGA titles. He wins the PGA Championship, bringing his total number of major wins to 12.

2007 Woods becomes a father in June when his wife, Elin, gives birth to a daughter.

GLOSSARY

birdie (BUR-dee) a score of one under par

bogey (BO-gee) a score of one over par

bunkers (BUHNGK-urz) obstructions on golf courses such as big sand traps

caddie (KA-dee) a person who assists a golfer, especially by carrying the golfer's bag of clubs

cut (KUHT) the elimination of players with the worst scores from competition; the cut is usually made after the first two rounds of play

discrimination (diss-krim-ih-NAY-shuhn) unfair treatment of a person or group based on race, gender, religion, or other factor

eagle (EE-guhl) a score of two under par

fairway (FAIR-way) the mowed part of the golf course between where a player tees off and the green

green (GREEN) the area right around the hole on a golf course

leaderboard (LEE-dur-bord) a big sign that lists the players in the order of their scores, with the leader at the top

par (PAR) a score that equals the expected number of strokes needed to put the ball in the hole; on most courses, that can be three to five strokes per hole

sports agents (SPORTS AY-junts) people who represent athletes and manage their personal appearances and endorsements

sports psychologist (SPORTS sye-KOL-uh-jist) a professional who helps athletes understand their mental strengths and weaknesses

sudden-death playoff (SUHD-uhn deth PLAY-awf) a tiebreaker; in golf, this means the first person to win a hole wins the match or tournament

tee shots (TEE SHOTS) shots that begin each hole; they are usually long drives that are aimed at the fairway

FOR MORE INFORMATION

Books

Doeden, Matt. *Tiger Woods (Sports Heroes and Legends)*.
Minneapolis: Lerner Publications, 2005.

Londino, Lawrence J. *Tiger Woods: A Biography*. Westport, CT: Greenwood Press, 2006.

Raatma, Lucia. *Tiger Woods (Trailblazers of the Modern World)*.
Milwaukee, WI: World Almanac Library, 2001.

Stewart, Mark. *Tiger Woods: Drive to Greatness*. Brookfield, CT: Millbrook Press, 2001.

Woods, Earl, and the Tiger Woods Foundation. *Start Something: You
Can Make a Difference*. New York: Simon and Schuster, 2000.

Web Sites

PGA Tour
www.pgatour.com/players/00/87/93/
Provides a profile of Tiger Woods

Tiger Woods
www.tigerwoods.com
Includes information about Woods's life and recent news, plus lots of photos

Tiger Woods Foundation
www.twfound.org
Offers information about the Tiger Woods Foundation and its mission

Tiger Woods Learning Center
www.twlc.org
Provides details about the Tiger Woods Learning Center and its mission

INDEX

birth, 5, 6
British Open, 11, 18, 26, 30, 32, 34
Buick Challenge, 22–23
Buick Invitational, 31, 32

caddies, 28, 37, 39
Canadian Open, 22
childhood, 7–11
Civil Rights Act (1964), 5
concentration, 7

discrimination, 5–6, 11, 16–18, 26, 40, 41

education, 10–11, 16
endorsements, 20–21, 26

Fred Haskins Award dinner, 22–24

goals, 11, 37, 42, 43
Golf Digest magazine, 8
Golf World magazine, 24
Grand Slam, 31
Greater Milwaukee Open, 22

Harmon, Butch, 13, 24, 26–27
Hogan, Ben, 28, 30
Hope, Bob, 8

International Management Group (IMG), 13

Los Angeles Open, 13–14

marriage, 32
Masters tournament, 11, 16–18, 24–26, 29, 31, 32, 37
meditation, 16

Nicklaus, Jack, 11, 30, 31, 32, 34, 39, 43
Nordegren, Elin, 32, 34

Optimist International Junior tournament, 11

Parnevik, Jesper, 32
PGA Championship, 11, 26, 28, 31, 34
Professional Golfers Association (PGA), 13–14

Quad City Classic, 22

Ryder Cup, 41, 42

sports agents, 13
Stanford University, 16, 18

Start Something program, 37

Tiger Jam concert, 39
Tiger Woods Design, 42
Tiger Woods Foundation, 35–36, 38, 39
Tiger Woods Learning Center, 36–37
training, 8–9, 13, 18, 21, 24, 26–27, 31

U.S. Amateur Championship, 18, 32
U.S. Junior Amateur Championship, 12, 13, 14–15, 32
U.S. Open, 11, 26, 29, 31–32, 34, 39
United States Golf Association (USGA), 12

wealth, 21, 32
Western Amateur tournament, 15
Williams, Steve, 28, 39
Woods, Earl, 6, 7, 13, 17, 24, 29, 33, 34
Woods, Kultida, 6, 8, 10, 13, 16, 33

ABOUT THE AUTHOR

Lucia Raatma was on vacation in April 1997 when Tiger Woods was gunning for his first win at the Masters. She found herself glued to a restaurant TV and didn't stop watching until he put on that green jacket. To her, watching golf and Tiger Woods is a real treat.

Over the years, Raatma has written a wide variety of books for young readers. Many are about character education and staying safe. Some of her favorites are about Queen Noor of Jordan, Jackie Robinson, John F. Kennedy, Jesse Owens, and Laura Ingalls Wilder.

She lives in New York with her husband, two children, and a golden retriever.